SANTA'S

sackful

of

1000

JOKES

Copyright © Michael Johnstone 1986

Published in Great Britain in 1991 by
World International Publishing Limited,
An Egmont Company, Egmont House, P.O. Box 111,
Great Ducie Street, Manchester M60 3BL.
Printed in Great Britain. ISBN 0 7235 4318 6

All rights reserved.

Contents

What?

What's red and goes 'Ho, ho, plop'?
  Father Christmas laughing his head off

What's black and white and flies?
  Supernun

What's green and camps?
  A boy sprout

What's best for for sick birds?
  Tweatment

What's the national anthem of the jungle?
  Tarzan Stripes Forever

What's got six legs and can't walk?
  Three pairs of trousers

What's served and never eaten?
  A tennis ball

What's sweet and swings from tree to tree?
  Tarzipan

What's Tarzan's favourite carol?
  Jungle bells

What's 300 metres tall, weighs 7,620 tonnes and is made of custard?
  The Trifle Tower

What's 300 metres tall, weighs 7,620 tonnes and attracts bees?
  The Eiffel Flower

What made the boy scout dizzy?
  Too many good turns

What's hot and moves at 100 miles an hour?
  A man running a temperature

What's got two legs and bursts into flames?
  Flared trousers

What's tight and good for water on the knee?
  Drainpipe trousers

What does a thief's son do?
  He takes after his father

What's the trampolinist's motto?
  'Life has it's ups and downs, but you can always bounce back'.

What's black, lives in Scotland and knew Eve?
  Tarmacadam

What's wrapped in silver foil and has an on/off switch?
  A television dinner

What's chocolate outside, peanut inside and sings hymns?
  A Sunday School Tweet

What's the best way to make trousers last?
  Wear the jacket first

What's the time when the clock strikes thirteen?
  Time to get a new clock

What's green, has two legs and a trunk?
  A seasick holiday-maker

What's good for stopping a person sleepwalking
  Tacks on the floor

What's white on the outside, pink in the middle and talks to itself?
  A tongue sandwich

What's the better fighter – a turnip or a chicken?
  A turnip – it's no chicken.

What's red and gives you the pips?
  A telephone box

What's a twitch?
  A nervous witch

What's a waiter's favourite sport?
  Tennis – it improves his service.

What's red, round and cheeky?
  Tomato sauce

What's brown and sneaks around the kitchen?
  Mince spies

What's grey and white and runs from London to Scotland without moving?
  The M1

What's Santa Claus's wife called?
  Mary Christmas

What's the best way to stop milk going sour?
  Drink it when it's fresh.

What's yellow and smells of bananas?
  A monkey that's been sick

What's got two legs, two arms and is good on a dark night?
  A light-headed man

What's big, bright and silly?
  A fool moon

What's good at adding and subtracting, and bumps into flames?
   A mothematician

What's John McEnroe's least favourite film?
   The Umpire Strikes Back

What's the best thing to do with a blue monster?
   Cheer him up.

What's the best thing to do with a green monster?
   Wait until he's ripe.

What's woolly, covered in chocolate and floats around the sun?
   A Mars baa

What's soft, sweet, white and comes from Mars?
   A Martian mallow

What's got forty-eight heads and no tails?
   A box of matches

What's grey, got whiskers and squeaks?
   A mouse on roller-skates

What's the best way to raise money?
   Lift it with a spoon.

What's good for helping you work, rest and die?
   A Mars Bar full of poison

What did Noah use to see in the dark?
   Floodlights

What's black and white and has four wheels?
   A nun on a skateboard

What's the best thing to do if your nose goes on strike?
    Pick-it.

What's four and five, if two's company and three's a crowd?
    Nine

What's awarded to designers of door-knockers?
    The No-bell prize

What happened when a lorry-load of hair restorer was spilt on the M1?
    Police combed the area.

What happened when ten beds were stolen from a warehouse?
    The police sprang into action.

What happened when someone drilled a hole in the nudist colony fence?
    The police looked into it.

What's got four legs and arrests criminals?
    A pair of nickers

What's bright red and thick?
    A blood clot

What's black and white, black and white, black and white, black and white?
    A nun falling downstairs

What's black and white and comes out of the oven spitting mad?
    A hot cross nun

What's black and white and goes up and down twenty times a day?
    A nun doing press-ups

What's brown and causes panic in a convent?
  A raised lavatory seat

What are long, pointed and run in families?
  Noses

What's red and runs at 100 miles an hour?
  The Bionic Nose

What's a dead man's nose called?
  The dead scenter

What's an operator?
  Someone who can't stand opera

What's black, white and red?
  A newspaper

What's black, hairy and surrounded by water?
  An oil wig

What's the dirtiest part of a ship?
  The officers' mess

What's round, white and giggles?
  A tickled onion

What's round, white and jumps around the garden?
  A spring onion

What's copper nitrate?
  A policeman's overtime

What's doughy and 50 metres high?
  The Leaning Tower of Pizza

What relation is a doorstep to a doormat?
  Step-farther

What do you get if you dial 666?
Australian policemen

What's yellow and white and travels at 2,000 miles an hour?
A Concorde pilot's egg sandwich

What's red, hunted and blows up buildings?
Guy Fox

What's the speed limit in Egypt?
60 Niles an hour

What's blue and white and full of fuzz?
A police car

What's a polygon?
A dead parrot

What's yellow, 'Miaows' and looks through windows?
A Peking Tom

What's white, round and smells?
A ping-ponging ball

What's a policeman with twenty children called?
'Daddy'

What's the best present for a man with everything?
Penicillin

What's red, spreads and shouldn't be broken?
A rash promise

What's politics?
A parrot that's swallowed an alarm clock

What's grey, lumpy and comes at you from four sides?
Quadraphonic porridge

What's red and white and full of policemen?
A sunburnt Panda

What's yellow, furry and rides along the sea-shore?
A peach buggy

What's a joiner's favourite TV show?
Plankety plank

What makes a piano laugh?
Someone tickling the ivories

What made the projector blush?
It saw the film strip.

What's yellow and fills fields with music?
Popcorn

What's an inkling?
A baby fountain-pen

What's the Pope's aeroplane called?
The Holy-copter

What's pink, got four legs and plays football?
Queen's Pork Rangers

What's feathered, clucks and wins Wimbledon?
Boris Pecker

What's made of pastry and good in emergencies?
  The quiche of life

What's blonde, sings and falls off stages?
  Wally Parton

What's the most popular gardening magazine in the world?
  Weeder's Digest

What's cold, Israeli and sells ice cream?
  Walls of Jericho

What's yellow and round, and 5 miles in circumference?
  The Great Ball of China

What's the wedding cake crying for?
  It can't stop shedding tiers.

What's a comedian's favourite motor-bike?
  A Yamaha-ha

What's got six feet and can't move?
  Two yards

What's a Grecian urn?
  About 500 drachmas a week

What's got long hair and weighs around 2 tonnes?
  A hippie-potamus

What's wet and says 'How do you do' sixteen times?
  Two octopuses shaking hands

What's covered in mud and runs back and forwards across zebra crossings?
  A dirty double-crosser

What's the time when you've toothache?
  Toth-hurty

What's as big as a rhinoceros and weighs nothing?
  A rhinoceros's shadow

What's a skeleton that sleeps all day called?
  Lazy bones

What's musical and steals?
  A robber breaking into song

What's an elastic-band thief called?
  A rubber bandit

What's a fatherless Rice Crispie?
  Snap, crackle – no pop

What's got four legs, glasses and is good for indigestion?
  The two Rennies

What's the best way to make a radio?
  Put three wires on a table; take one away – you've a
  wireless.

What's a fjord?
  A Scandinavian motor car

What's clever, sweet and travels by underground?
  A tube of Smarties

What keeps sheep warm in winter?
  Central bleating

What happened when the Scotsman washed his kilt?
  He couldn't do a fling with it.

Danger! Cannibals, ghosts and witches

What's a cannibal's favourite breakfast?
  Baked beings on toast

What's a cannibal's favourite game?
  Swallow my leader

What did the cannibal say to the missionary?
  'Dr Livingstone, I consume.'

What does a cannibal's wife make for dinner?
  Good soup – if she's cooked properly

What do cannibals eat at parties?
  Buttered host

What's a sandwich man?
  A cannibal's packed lunch

What do cannibal girls look for in their husbands?
  Not a lot – as long as they're edible

What did the cannibal say when she saw a sleeping missionary?
  'Oh look! Breakfast in bed.'

What's a contented cannibal?
  Someone who's fed up with people

What's the highlight of a cannibal wedding?
  Toasting the happy couple

What's Count Dracula's favourite coffee?
  De-coffin-ated

What do you get if you cross Dracula with Sir Lancelot?
  A bite in shining armour

What's got feathers, wings and fangs?
  Count Duckula

What's Dracula's car called?
  A mobile blood unit

What do you get if you cross Dracula with snow?
  Frostbite

What do famous vampires get on their birthdays?
  Fangmail

What's a graveyard?
  The dead centre of the town

What's hot, meaty and eaten by ghosts?
  Ghoulash

What did the father ghost say to his son?
  'Don't spook until you're spooken to.'

What's pink, hoinks and drinks blood?
  A hampire

What's Count Dracula's New York house called?
  The Vampire State Building

What do you get if you cross a policeman with a ghost?
  An inspectre

What did King Kong say to the Empire State Building?
  'Mummy!'

What's wrapped in Clingfilm and lives in bell towers?
  The Lunchpack of Notre Dame

What makes vampire families stick together?
  Blood is thicker than water.

What's a vampire's favourite fruit?
  A necktarine

What's a vampire's second favourite fruit?
  A blood orange

What's a vampire's favourite song?
  'Fangs For The Memory'

. . . and his favourite soup?
  Scream of tomato

What do witches have for breakfast?
  Snap, cackle and pop

What's a cannibal who has eaten his mother's sister?
  An aunt-eater

What's a vegetarian cannibal's favourite food?
  Swedes

What's a vampire bath?
  A bat tub

What's a vampire's favourite animal?
  A giraffe

What's invisible and plays football?
  A ghoulie

What's spooky and ruled France?
  Charles de Ghoul

What weighed 20 stone and terrorized Paris?
   The Fat-tum of the Opera

What's a missionary's ambition?
   To give cannibals a taste of Christianity

What's a ghost doctor?
   A surgical spirit

What's a cannibal's favourite meal?
Snake and pygmy pie

At cross purposes

What's a cross between an ambassador and a rug called?
  A diplomat

What do you get if you cross a famous detective with a bubble bath?
  Sherlock Foams

What's a skeleton in a kilt called?
  Bony Prince Charlie

What do you get if you cross a chicken with a cement-mixer?
  A brick layer

What do you get if you cross bacon with a space ship?
  An unidentified frying object

What do you get if you cross a woodwind instrument with an ancient Briton?
  An anglo-saxophone

What do you get if you cross a car with a book . . . ?
  An autobiography

. . . and a young donkey with a naked charlady?
  An asset stripper

What do you get if you cross the Atlantic with the Titanic?
About 200 miles off the coast of Newfoundland

What do you get if you cross a camera with a crocodile?
A snap shot

What do you get if you cross a worm with a fur coat?
A caterpillar

What do you get if you cross a chicken with a guitar?
A hen that makes music when you pluck it

What do you get if you cross a screwdriver with a cat . . . ?
A tool kitty

. . . and a spaniel, a poodle and a rooster?
A cockerpoodledoo

What do you get if you cross a cow, a sheep and a baby goat?
The Milky Baa Kid

What do you get if you cross a cow with an octopus?
An animal that milks itself

What do you get if you cross a cat with a canary?
A satisfied cat and a dead canary

What do you get if you cross a chicken with a torch?
A battery hen

What do you get if you cross a jeep with a dog?
A land rover

What do you get if you cross a donkey with its mother . . . ?
  Ass-ma

. . . or a spaniel with a firefly?
  A dog with night vision

What do you get if you cross an elephant with a mouse?
  Enormous holes in the skirting-board

What do you get if you cross an elephant with a canary?
  A very messy cage

What do you get if you cross a plumber with a jeweller?
  A ring around the bath

What do you get if you cross a rug with a banana?
  A carpet slipper

What do you get if you cross a monkey with a flower?
  A chimp-pansy

What do you get if you cross a cat with an ambulance man?
  A first-aid kitty

What do you get if you cross a horse with a footballer?
  A centaur-forward

What do you get if you cross a pig with Busby?
  Crackling on the line

What do you get if you cross an Italian with a Scots mist?
  Roman in the gloamin'

21

What do you get if you cross a jar of jam with an elephant?
  Sandwiches that don't forget

What do you get if you cross an elephant with a kangaroo?
  Huge holes all over Australia

What do you get if you cross a chicken with a kangaroo?
  Pouched eggs

What do you get if you cross a motorway with an elephant?
  Run over

What do you get if you cross a chicken with gunpowder?
  An eggsplosion

What do you get if you cross a Muppet with the mist?
  Kermit the fog

What do you get if you cross an elephant with a pigeon?
  Dirty bus queues

What do you get if you cross a hovercraft with an elf?
  A cross-channel fairy

What do you get if you cross a tape-measure with a steam-roller?
  Flat feet

What do you get if you cross a giraffe with a dog?
  An animal that barks at aeroplanes

What do you get if you cross a Hawaiian dancer with an Indian brave?
  A hula whoop

What do you get if you cross a black hat with a jet engine?
  A fast bowler

What do you get if you cross a bee with a half-kilo of mince?
  Humburgers

What do you get if you cross an elephant with a crow?
  Lots of broken telegraph poles

What do you get if you cross a river with a boat?
  To the other side

What do you get if you cross a daffodil with a calculator?
  A flower with square roots

What do you get if you cross an hyaena with a dumb owl?
  An animal that no one likes, and which doesn't give a hoot

What do you get if you cross a plum with a tiger?
  A purple people-eater

What do you get if you cross a jogger with a beach?
  Quicksand

What do you get if you cross an aeroplane with a peach tart?
  Pie in the sky

What do you get if you cross a railway station with Lady
Godiva?
  Paddington Bare

What do you get if you cross a chicken with a bottle of
whisky?
  Scotch eggs

What do you get if you cross a hamburger with a Scotsman?
  A Big Mac

What do you get if you cross a top with a puppet?
  Spinocchio

What do you get if you cross a bulb with a frog?
A croakus

What do you get if you cross a camel with a rose?
A flower that never needs watering

What do you get if you cross an invader with a cake?
Attila the Bun

What do you get if you cross a horse with a skunk?
Whinny the Pooh

What do you get if you cross a python with a saxophone?
A snake in the brass

PARP!

What's that?

What's white on the outside and acts badly?
A ham sandwich

What's white on the ouside and tells rotten jokes?
A corny beef sandwich

What's sniffy and plays rock music?
Electric catarrh

What lies in the gutter and moans loudly?
A car with a broken windscreen

What would you get if all the cars in the USA were red?
A red carnation

What did the cashier say when he was caught stealing?
'I thought the change would do me good.'

What's frozen and covered with grass?
A common cold

What's black, shiny and serves drinks?
A crowbar

What's wooden and smells?
A high chair

What's the best way of making a dead dog float?
Take a scoop of dead dog and a scoop of ice cream.

What's Denice's brother called?
De nephew

What's white and drives up the M1 in reverse?
An Englishman who knows the *Highway Code*
backwards

What's fat and lives in China?
A chunk

What's warm, greasy and romantic?
Chips that pass in the night

What do you say to a legless dog?
'Draggies!'

What's crunchy and lives in the Middle East?
Sultan Vinegar crisps

What's yellow and goes 'Boo-hoo splash'?
A Chinaman crying his eyes out

What has two legs, rides a broomstick, goes to the
seaside, and won't go in the water?
A chicken sand-witch

What's a computer's favourite food?
Silicon chips

'What made the chicken cross the road?'
  'I don't know. What made the chicken cross the road?'
  'I'm not sure, but I suppose he had a fowl reason.'

What's an Eskimo cow called?
An Eski-moo

What's red and comes out of the ground at 100 miles an hour?
  An E-type carrot

What's an American cow called?
  A Moo Yorker

What's a vampire's goodnight kiss?
Necking

What's a bad-tempered needlework teacher called?
  A proper sew-and-sew

What's a flatterer?
  Someone who lives in a high-rise block

What's the punishment for bigamy?
Two mothers-in-law

What's the best way to save water?
Dilute it.

What's the best way to stop people writing on bus shelters?
Make the buses run on time.

What's a guillotine?
A French chopping centre

What's poverty?
Watching the world go buy

What has feathers and drives on the motorway?
Coq-au-van

What's green, big and doesn't speak all day?
The Incredible Sulk

What's famous and lives in lavatories?
Someone flushed with success

What has a bowler hat and umbrella, and crawls?
A civil serpent

What's a glue-covered aspirin good for?
A man with a splitting headache

What's plastic, works on batteries, and counts cattle?
  A cow-culator

What's yellow, round, and bleeds in New York gutters?
  John Lemon

What's green and for hire?
  A taxi cabbage

What's yellow and stuffs cabs?
  A Chinese taxidermist

What's green, sour, and cleans teeth?
  A tooth pickle

What's worse than raining cats and dogs?
Hailing a taxi

What's yellow and explodes on your pudding?
  Kamikaze custard

What's cowardly, thin and full of noodles?
  Chicken soup

What's dark, talks with a Scots accent and goes 'Tick tock'?
  The Black Watch

What's red and green, and sits in the garden going 'Tick tock, tick tock?'
  A metrognome

What's the easiest way to make a bandstand?
  Take the chairs away.

What's red, squashy, and says 'pardon'?
  A polite strawberry with hiccups

What's white, runs, and lies under the bed with its
tongue hanging out?
  A sneaker

What's a signature?
  A baby swan's autograph

What's the best way to start a pudding race?
  Sago

What's a sick duck?
  A malardy

What colour is a shout?
  Yell-oh

What has feathers and carries water?
  An aqua-duck

What do sheep look for at the sales?
  Baagains

What's a lazy shoe called?
  A loafer

What has eight eyes, a tongue, and tells tales?
  A sneaker

What's bent, salty, and sings rock songs?
  Elvis Pretzel

What's brown, lumpy, and given to actors and
actresses?
  Acadamy awarts

What's yellow, has twenty-four legs, and sings?
  Twelve canaries

What's a Scots chef called?
  Dinner Ken

What's green, noisy and dangerous?
  A thundering herd of cucumbers

What's a ghost's favourite dinner?
  Spookhetti

What's a ghost's favourite breakfast?
  Dreaded wheat

What's mad and travels to the moon?
  A luny module

What's sweet, sour, dangerous, and travels?
  Take-away kung food

What's green, wears a black cloak, and holds up stage-
coaches?
  Dick Gherkin

What's brown and travels at 110 miles an hour?
  A fuel-injected potato

What's brown, round, and travels at 1,000 miles an
hour?
  An intercontinental ballistic rissole

What goes 'Ha ha, aaaagh . . .'?
  Someone killing himself with laughter

What's a volcano?
A mountain that keeps being sick

What makes a Maltese Cross?
A kick in the stomach

What's an Irishman who keeps bouncing off walls
called?
Rick O'Shea

What's a sleeping prehistoric monster called?
A dinosnore

What's white and runs through the desert with a
bedpan?
Florence of Arabia

What's pink and grows under your nose?
Tulips

What's long and green and goes 'Hith, hith'?
A snake with a lisp

What's purple and swings through the trees in the
jungle?
Tarzan of the Grapes

What's worse than a giraffe with bad bronchitis?
A centipede with athlete's foot

What's good for drawing teeth painlessly?
A pencil

What's the best way of preventing diseases caused by biting fleas?
Don't bite fleas.

What's a small Indian guitar called?
A baby sitar

What's a bad German fighter-pilot called?
Baron von Wrecked Often

What's thick and works in a florists shop?
A blooming idiot

What has two legs and talks behind your back?
A barber

What has two legs and inspects rabbit-holes?
The burrow surveyor

What's yellow, has twenty-two legs and two wings?
A Chinese football team

What's a miser vegetarian's greatest dilemma?
Free meat

What's a man with no legs called?
Neil (kneel)

What's a one-legged girl called?
  Eileen (I lean)

What's brown on both sides and 200 metres high?
  The Toast Office Tower

What has five fingers and drives a tractor?
  A farm hand

What's a man with a spade in the head called?
  Doug

What's a cow's favourite holiday resort?
  Moo Zealand

What's right and never wrong?
  An angle

What's an astronaut's favourite meal?
  Launch

What's an archaeologist?
  Someone who's career is in ruins

What's a troupe of fat actors called?
  A broad cast

What's the first thing a ball does when it stops rolling?
  It looks round.

What's brown and digs holes when it's fast asleep?
  A bull-dozer

What's blue, worn over a shirt, and bursts into flames easily?
   A blazer

What made the biscuit box?
   It saw the rum punch.

What's a biplane?
   The last words a pilot says before he bales out

What happened to the two blood clots who fell in love?
   They loved in vein

What's smashing and comes between morning and afternoon?
   A lunchtime break

What's 36 inches long and popular with children?
   Blue Metre

What's hot, greasy, and steals cattle?
   A beef burglar

What's smelly and hums?
   Beethoven's remains decomposing

What does a 6-foot tall, red-haired, green-shoed butcher weigh?
  Meat

What's brown and white, and runs around the forest crying 'Mummy, Mummy'?
  Bambi

What's white, creamy, and always comes back to you?
  A boo-meringue

What has two legs and sits in a bacon slicer?
  A butcher getting behind in his deliveries

What's yellow and brown and dances round toadstools?
  A brownie with jaundice

What's the best day to cook bacon and eggs?
  Fry-day

What was Ann Boleyn's last meal?
  Two cold chops

What's boring and moves from branch to branch carrying a briefcase?
  A bank manager

What's furry and worn by nudists?
  Bear skins

What's a bore?
  Someone with nothing to say who says it

What's the shortest bridge in the world?
  The bridge on your nose

What's green and travels at 120 miles an hour?
  An Austin Healey Sprout

What's a man who buys and sells flies called?
An ant-tic dealer

What's pink and white, sharp, and served before a meal?
A-per-i-tif

What's tall, dark and hamsome?
A very bad actor

What would you shout if you fell off the Matterhorn?
'A-a-a-a-a-l-p

What's black and goes 'ABC . . . slurp . . . DEF . . . slurp?'
An African eating alphabet soup

What's wet and comes out of the bottle at 100 miles an hour?
An Aston Martini

What's an ant that's written a book called?
The author

What's got four wheels and sizzles when it's hot?
An old banger

What's an army?
The thingie up your sleevy

What's a hippie?
The thingie your leggies hang from

What's the best cure for acid indigestion?
Stop drinking acid.

What was Noah's profession?
Ark-itect

What's two rows of cabbages called?
  A dual cabbage-way

What happened to the cowardly human canonball?
  He got fired

What's brown and squeaks when covered with milk?
  Mice crispies

What's meaty, bony, and stands at an angle?
  A lean chop

What's blue, green, yellow, purple, brown, black and
white, and good on the draw?
  A box of crayons

What's small, blue and eats cakes?
  A blue dwarf cake-eater

What's the best way to make a cigarette lighter?
  Take out some of the tobacco.

What's green and jumps up and down?
  A lettuce at a discothèque

What's 3 feet tall and rides on the Paris subway?
  Another Metro-gnome

What's brown and fills policeman's sandwiches?
  Truncheon meat

What's soft, wet and sings?
  Chamois Davis Junior

What's black, sweet, and makes history lessons
interesting?
  Dates

What's white, dropped by birds, and angers drivers?
  A deposit on a new car

What's round, rough and deeply in love?
  Swedehearts

What's a spaceman's watch?
  A lunartic

What's a midget novelist called?
  A short story writer

What's a snowflake's dance called?
  A snowball

What's red, blue and staggers?
  Stupor Man

What's the only thing to eat on a desert island?
  The sandwiches there (sand which is there - *geddit*!)

What's locked up and wears a thermos on his head?
  The Man in the Iron Flask

What's got two legs, makes movies, and jumps over
trees?
  John Tree-Vaulter

What's the best way of stopping sea-sickness?
  Bolt your food down.

What's pink and white, comes out at night, and sings in
a high voice?
  Falsetto teeth

What's a twain?
  What a wabbit wides on the wailway

What's Batman doing in the tree?
  Looking for Robin's nest

Animal crackers

What's yellow and succeeds?
   A toothless canary

What's the wasps' favourite TV channel?
   The Bee-Bee C

What's grey, hairy, and makes animals yawn?
   A wild bore

What's a mad blackbird called?
   A raven lunatic

What do you get if you cross an insect and a rabbit?
   Bugs Bunny

What's a bee?
   An insect that stings for its supper

What do bees do with honey?
   Cell it

What do you get if you pour boiling water down a rabbit-hole?
   Hot cross bunnies

What did the bees go on strike for?
   Shorter flowers and more honey

What has 100 legs and flies?
   Fifty dead birds

What's left after the lawnmower runs over a bird?
  Shredded tweat

What's smaller than a mite's mouth?
  A mite's teeth

What's grey, has sharp teeth, and holds up socks?
  An alligarter

What lies on the ground 100 feet in the air?
  A dead centipede

What's a cow after she gives birth?
  De-calf-inated

What's white when it goes into the water and brown
when it comes out?
  A labrador on a snowy day

What's a cat's favourite newspaper?
  Mews of the world

What's brown, got three humps, and lives in the desert?
  A camel with a rucksack

What's yellow and goes 'tick tock, tick tock'?
  A clockwork canary

What's white, fluffy and floats?
  A cat-emeringue

What do you get if you cross a cow with a camel?
  Lumpy milk shakes

What has five legs and gives milk?
  A three-legged cow and a milk-maid

What has 100 legs and goes in one ear and out the other?
  A centipede in a cornfield

What's a three-humped camel called?
   Humphrey

What's black and white and green and brown?
   A cow with a runny nose in a muddy field

What's yellow and goes 'Phut . . . phut . . . phut. . .'?
   An outboard canary

What's spotted and untrustworthy?
   A cheetah

What's black, sits in trees, and is highly dangerous?
   A crow with a machine-gun

What goes 'Cluck, cluck . . . BANG'?
   A chicken in a minefield

What made the chicken run?
   It saw the fox trot

What's a lazy rooster?
   A cockle-doodle don't

What's green, furry and turns into a 5-tonne truck?
   A caterpillar tractor

What's yellow, sings, and weighs a tonne?
   Two half-tonne canaries

What's yellow, stands in a river during a storm and
doesn't get wet?
   A duck with an umbrella

What's white with black and red spots?
   A dalmation with measles

What's yellow and goes 'kcauq, kcauq'?
    A duck flying backwards

What's 'Quack, quack?'
    Double ducks

What do you get if you cross a cow with a duck?
    Cream quackers

What's blue and barks?
    A dog in a plastic bag

What's green and doesn't bark?
    The same dog a month later

What's a stupid donkey?
    An animal that makes an ass of itself

What has four legs, barks, and plays tennis?
    John McEn-rover

What has four legs, barks and dances?
    Natalia Maka-rover

What do you get if you cross an elephant with a mouse?
    Scared cats

What's good for measuring dogs?
    A barking metre

What's a cat that has just swallowed a duck?
    A duck-filled fatty-puss

What would you call a bad-tempered gorilla with cotton
wool in its ears?
    Anything you want; it can't hear you

'What do you get if you cross a mynah bird with a lion?'
'I don't know. What do you get if you cross a mynah
bird with a lion?'
'Neither do I. But if it speaks to you, you'd better
listen.'

What's brown, has four legs and a trunk?
A mouse coming back from holiday

What's a Scots parrot?
A MacCaw

What's a cow's favourite TV show?
Dr Moo

What's green and turns red at the flick of a switch?
A frog in an electric blender

What's white one minute and brown the next?
A white rat in a microwave

What's brown one minute and white the next?
A brown rat in the deep freeze

What's green and makes a loud noise?
  A frog horn

What do frogs wear in summer?
  Open-toad sandals

What's a frog's favourite drink?
  Croaka-Cola

What's green and stands in the corner?
  A naughty frog

What has four legs, flies, and cries a lot?
  A mother flea watching her children going to the dogs

What do you get if you cross a giraffe with a hedgehog?
  A very long toothbrush

What makes a giraffe so arrogant?
  It finds it hard to swallow its pride.

What's a hedgehog's favourite lunch?
  Prickled onions

What's best for a sick horse?
  A visit to the horspital

What's a horse's favourite game?
  Stable tennis

What's best for a kangaroo with appendicitis?
  A hoperation

What's sweet and lives in the jungle?
  A meringue-utang

What's grey and out of bounds?
  An exhausted kangaroo

What has antlers and frightens cats?
  Mickey Moose

What's the fastest growing animal?
  A kangaroo – it grows in leaps and bounds.

What's black and white, striped, and lives at the North Pole?
  A lost zebra

What's a kangaroo's favourite year?
  A leap year

What's black and white, gives milk, and cuts grass?
  A lawn moo-er

What's a louse's favourite party?
  A louse-warming party

'What's green, has ten legs and huge teeth?'
  'I don't know. What's green, has ten legs and huge teeth?'
  'I don't know either. But whatever it is, it's crawling up your back!'

What's brown, whiskered and cuts grass?
  A lawn miaow-er

What do mice do all day?
  Mousework

What's a mouse's favourite game?
  Hide and squeak

What has four legs and eats off the floor?
  A horse with bad stable manners

What's brightly coloured and goes 'Hmmmmmmm-choo, hmmmmmmm-choo'?
  A humming-bird with a bad cold

What's covered in feathers and cracks jokes?
  A comedi-hen

What's green and prickly?
  A seasick hedgehog

What has a head, a tail, four legs, and sees equally well in either direction?
  A blind horse

What's slithery and good at counting?
  An adder

What does a skunk do when it's angry?
  It raises a stink.

What did one skunk say to another skunk?
  'Let us spray'

What's a termite's favourite breakfast?
  Oak meal

What do frogs fly flags from?
  Tadpoles

What's grey and full of ducks?
  Madame Tussaud's Quacks Works

What's grey, buzzes, and eats cheese?
  A mouse-quito

What's a cat's favourite TV show?
  Mews at Ten

What's grey, got twelve legs and can't see?
  Three blind mice

What's grey, squeaks and weighs 4 tonnes?
  A mouse built to government plans

What's grey, weighs 12 stone and says 'Here kitty, kitty'?
  A 12-stone mouse

What's Miss Piggy's favourite perfume?
  Vinegar and honey. (Kermit likes sweet-and-sour pork)

What's grey, squeaks and ruled Rome?
  Julius Cheeser

What's furry, stings, collects nectar, and is difficult to hear?
  A mumble bee

What's black and white and spins round at 60 miles an hour?
  A penguin in a cement-mixer

What's made of straw and full of milk bottles?
  A cow's nest

What do you call a 3,000-pound orang-utan?
  'Sir!'

What did the octopus give his wife for Christmas?
  Four pairs of gloves

What makes an octopus a good fighter?
  He's very well armed.

What's grey and sits in a tree singing 'Hoots mon, hoots mon'?
  A Scottish owl

What's creamy and good for sick pigs?
  Oinkment

What do pandas take on holiday?
  The bear essentials

What's pink and writes to pigs?
  A pig's pen-friend

What's two hedgehogs called?
  A prickly pair

What's a two-week-old, black-and-white Russian dog called?
  A puppy

What's furry, has whiskers and chases outlaws?
  A posse cat

What's black and white and makes a dreadful noise?
  A penguin playing the bagpipes

What's feathered and sings 'Pieces of four! Pieces of four!'?
  Short John Silver's parrot

What do porcupines say when they're kissing?
  'Ouch!'

What's black, barks and runs in the gutter?
  A poddle after it's been raining cats and dogs

What's small, blind, furry and seen on television at lunchtime?
  Pebble Mole at One

What has two legs, a big beak, and hops?
  A pelicangaroo

What good's reindeer?
  'It makes the grass grow – sweetie!'

What's the best way to catch a squirrel?
  Climb a tree and act like a nut.

What has four legs, flies, and tells tales?
  A stool pigeon

What's pink and can't stand still?
  A pig in a tumble-drier

What's wooden, howls and is dangerous?
  A timber wolf

What's green, spicy and pecks trees?
  Woody Wood Pickle

What's a woodpecker with no beak?
  A headbanger

What's got four legs, barks, and goes 'Tick tock'?
  A watch dog

What's the worm army called?
  The apple corps

What's black and white and runs on sixteen wheels?
  A zebra on roller-skates

What's black and red and runs on sixteen wheels?
  A sunburnt zebra on roller-skates

What's black and white and stops buses?
  A zebra crossing

What do you get if you cross a zebra with a pig?
  Striped sausages

What do you get if you cross a centipede with a mynah bird?
  A walkie-talkie

What has twelve legs and plays football in a saucer?
  Two flies, practising for the Cup

What has feathers, flies and can lift elephants?
  A crane

What's the best way to talk to a man-eating tiger?
  By long-distance telephone

What's extinct and works in rodeos?
    A bronco-saurus

What's 50 foot long and jumps every two seconds?
    A dinosaur with hiccups

What would you get if you crossed a dinosaur with a witch?
    A tyrannosaurus hex

What's got feathers and goes 'C.c.c.c.c.c.c.c.c.c.c.c.c.c. . .'?
    A rooster with a bad stutter

What's the best way to catch a rabbit?
    Hide in a bush and make a noise like a lettuce.

What's a sheep's hairdresser called?
    A baa-baa shop

What's a pig's favourite ballet?
    Swine Lake

What's hairy, barks and flies?
    A Skye terrier

What's a myth?
    An unmarried female moth

What has six legs, bites, and talks in code?
    A morse-quito

What makes Donald Duck fall over?
    Disney spells

What's yellow, comes from Peru and is completely unknown?
    Euston Bear

What's red and green and jumps out of aeroplanes?
    A parrot-trooper

What's grey, squeaks and hangs around in caves?
    Stalagmice

What's suntanned, quacks and runs his country single-handed?
    A South American duck-tator

What's a spider that has just got married?
    A newly-web

What's brown, quacks and is full of words?
    A duck-tionary

What's grey, heavy and sends people to sleep?
    A hypnopotamus

What's brown, has four legs and a yellow beak, and barks?
    A duckshund

What's brown, quacks and robs safes?
    A safe quacker

What's furry, miaows, and chases mice underwater?
    A catfish

What has twelve legs, six ears and one eye?
    Three blind mice and half a goldfish

What's white and turns cartwheels?
    A white horse pulling a cart

What's green, sits on a lily pad and sings 'Cloak, cloak'?
    A Chinese flog

What purrs along the motorway and leaves holes in the lawn?
    A Moles Royce

What's a wombat for?
    Playing wom

What's a bald koala bear called?
    Fred Bare

Plummeting the depths

What's brown and yellow and flies along the bottom of the sea?
  A bee in a submarine

What's long, lives underwater, and likes Latin American music?
  A conga eel

What fish never swims?
  A dead one

What fish do shoemakers use everyday?
  Soles and eels

What's battery-powered and good for deaf fish?
  A herring aid

What's brown, lives underwater and sleeps all day?
  Jack the Kipper

What's got sharp teeth, chops down cherry trees and never tells lies?
  Jaws Washington

What did the kipper say to the doctor?
  'I'm here to be cured.'

What's 10 metres long, lives in Scotland, and never wins anything?
  The Luck Less Monster

What's yellow and never talks to anyone?
  A lemon sole

What do you get if you cross a sardine with a sabre?
  A swordfish

What's made of chocolate, and rolls along the sea bed?
  An oyster egg

What's the most famous fish?
  The starfish

What lives underwater, has tentacles and is quick on the draw?
  Billy the Squid

What has tentacles and dances on television?
  The Squids from *Fame*

What's blue, has sharp teeth and sings?
  Boy Jaws

What made the sand wet?
  The see wee'ed.

What's grey, lives on the beach, and talks a lot?
  Mussel Harty

What's silvery, swims in shoals and goes 'Dot, dash, dot, dot'?
  Morse cod

What's red and scared of Captain Ahab?
  Moby Bus

What's black and comes out of the North Sea swearing?
  Crude oil

What's black and comes out of the North Sea saying 'Pardon me'?
  Refined oil

What's pink, lives on the sea bed, and croons?
  Frankie Prawn

What's grey and wears a crown?
  The Prince of Whales

What's pink, lives on the sea bed, and is highly dangerous?
  Al Caprawn

What's three years old, has tentacles and wants to live on land?
  A crazy mixed-up squid

What's blue, and chewed by whales?
  Blubber gum

What's a baby whale called?
  A little blubber

What sits on the sea bed and shakes?
  A nervous wreck

What's the best way to talk to a fish?
  Drop it a line.

What sits at the bottom of the sea and makes you an offer you can't refuse?
  The Cod Father

What's shiny and roars along the sea bed at 100 miles an hour?
  A motorpike

Vive la difference

What's the difference between a boxer and a man with a cold?
   One knows his blows: the other blows his nose.

What's the difference between a bus driver and a cold?
   One knows the stops: the other stops the nose.

What's the difference between a train and a tree?
   One leaves its shed: the other sheds its leaves.

What's the difference between a telegraph pole and Joan of Arc?
   One is made of wood: the other is Maid of Orleans.

What's the difference between a well-dressed man and a tired dog?
   The man wears a suit: the dog just pants.

What's the difference between an umbrella and a chatterbox?
   You can shut an umbrella up.

What's the difference between a coyote and a flea?
   One howls on the prairie: the other prowls on the hairy.

'What's the difference between a biscuit and a cow?'
   'I don't know. What is the difference?'
   'Have you ever tried dunking a cow in your tea?'

What's the difference between a canoe and a Scotsman?
   A canoe tips – sometimes.

What's the difference between a blind man and a sailor in jail?
   One can't see to go: the other can't go to sea.

What's the difference between a dog and a flea?
   A dog can have fleas: have you ever heard of a flea having dogs?

What's the difference between a man bitten by a mosquito and a man going on holiday?
One is going to itch: the other is itching to go

'What's the difference between an elephant and a letter box?
'I don't know. What's the difference?'
'Remind me never to ask you to post a letter for me'.

What's the difference between a photocopying machine and a flu epidemic?
One makes facsimilies: the other makes sick families.

What's the difference between a married man and a bachelor?
One kissed his missus: the other misses his kisses.

What's the difference between a market gardener and an actor?
One minds his peas: the other minds his cues.

What's the difference between a moulting dog and a painter?
One sheds his coat: the other coats his shed.

What's the difference between someone *going* up a staircase and someone *looking* up a staircase?
One steps up the stairs: the other stares up the steps.

'What's the difference between a pitchfork and a toothpick?'
'I don't know. What is the difference between a pitchfork and a toothpick?'
'Well, if you don't take that pitchfork out of your mouth, you'll hurt yourself.

What's the difference between love and marriage?
   Marriage is forever.

What's the difference between the law and an ice cube?
   Nothing. They're both just-ice!

What's the difference between a seamstress and a nurse?
   One cuts dresses: the other dresses cuts.

What's the difference between a burglar and a man with a
wig?
   One has false keys: the other has false locks.

What's the difference between a ball and a prince?
   One is thrown in the air: the other is heir to the throne.

What's the difference between 16 ounces and a pianist?
   One weighs a pound: the other pounds away.

What's the difference between the Prince of Wales and a
mother gorilla?
   One is the heir apparent: the other is a hairy parent.

What's the difference between a beer can and a silly
Dutchman?
   One is a hollow cylinder: the other is a silly Hollander.

What's the difference between a buffalo and a bison?
   You can't wash in a buffalo.

What's the difference between a destroyer and a cheat?
   One rules the waves: the other waives the rules.

What's the difference between a squeeze and a louse?
   One is a bear hug: the other is a hair bug.

What's the difference between a healthy rabbit and an odd
person?
   One is a fit bunny: the other is a bit funny.

What's that again

What's alcoholic and heavy?
A gin and cement

What's yellow and stupid?
Thick custard

What's cold and comes in tins?
Chilli-beans

What happened when the cat swallowed a ball of wool?
She had mittens

What's dishonest and coated in cement?
A hardened criminal

What's the best way to keep Britain tidy?
Send all your rubbish to France

What's found in some cups and can never get out?
A crack

'What's green, round, grows in fields and has four wheels?'
'I don't know. What is green, round, grows in fields and
has four wheels?'
'A cabbage. I lied about the wheels.'

What's round, toothed and bites?
A vicious circle

What stopped the sailors playing cards?
The captain stood on the deck.

What's Camelot known for?
Its good knight life

What's white on the outside and scares easily?
A chicken sandwich

What's served in glasses and difficult to swallow?
  A stiff drink

What's the laziest letter in the alphabet?
  'E', because it's always in bed

What makes young Egyptians good children?
  They hold their mummies in deep respect.

What does an elf do after school?
  Gnome work

What's black, shrivelled and hangs from the ceiling?
  A careless electrician

What's a chicken's favourite cake?
  A layer cake

What's the best thing to do if your cat swallows a
dictionary?
  Take the words right out of its mouth.

What makes cooks cruel?
  They beat eggs and batter fish

What's a karate expert's favourite meal?
  Chops

What makes a doctor angry?
  Running out of patients

What's painful and makes holes in the ground?
  A rheumatic drill

What's a doctor who melts in the sun called?
    A plastic surgeon

What do twins speak in Holland?
    Double Dutch

What has two legs and goes 'Put, put, put, put, put, put'?
    A very bad golfer

What's smelly and spoken in Scotland?
    Garlic

What has 750,000 people and is totally deserted?
    Glasgow on a flag day

What's the best way to stop children jumping up and down
in bed?
    Put Super Glue on the ceiling

What do jelly babies wear on their feet?
    Gum boots

What's gegs?
    Scrambled eggs

What's Mr and Mrs Fortune's daughter called?
    Miss Fortune

What swims and gives milk?
    A milk float

What's a miser's first reaction when his house catches fire?
    To pray for rain

What's the fastest drink?
    Milk: it's pasteurised before you see it.

What's always flying and never goes anywhere?
A flag

What's the hottest show on television?
Flame

What's white on the outside, green in the middle and jumps?
A frog sandwich

What's the best way to get rid of excess fat?
Divorce him.

What's made of wood, sails and grants wishes?
A ferry godmother

What has twenty-two legs and goes 'Crunch, crunch, crunch'?
A football team eating crisps

What's the best butter in the world?
A goat

What's the most slippery country in the world?
Greece

What's pink and wrinkly and belongs to grandma?
Grandpa

What makes grass so dangerous?
All those blades

What's a cheerful flee called?
A hoptimist

What has six legs, four eyes and a tail?
A horse and rider

What's round, tasty and lifts weights?
  An extra-strong mint

What stays hot in the fridge?
Mustard

What's got 500 legs and can't walk?
Half a millipede

What happened when the fish fought the chips?
  The fish got battered.

What do frogs sit on?
Toadstools

What exams do farmers take?
Hay levels

What's a fisherman paid?
The net profits

What's alive when it's fed and dead when it's watered?
  A fire

What do you get if you dial 01-493-893948949298998989?
  A very sore finger

What's furry, rides a motor bike and jumps buses?
Evel the Weavel

What's green and sings?
Elvis Parsley

What's the best way to make an egg roll?
Push it down hill.

What did the Six Million Dollar Man do when he lost at
cards?
  He threw his hand in.

What did the Spanish farmer say to his chickens?
'Olé!'

What's a 2-foot high comic?
A half wit

What's a Frenchman's breakfast?
Huit heures bix

What's a Hindu?
Lay eggs

What gets larger the more you subtract?
A hole

What comes out of the washing machine at 100°C?
Hot pants

What has four legs, a tail, runs at 30 miles an hour and is seventy years old?
An old-age pension-hair

What has four wheels and is full of rabbits?
A hutch-back car

What's yellow, runny and shocking?
Electric honey

What's 6 foot tall, weighs 12 stone and can hold up planes?
A hi-jacker

What's smelly and comes out firing guns?
A septic tank

What's small, brown and carries a suitcase?
   A handle

What has two legs and lives in a cement mixer?
   A hard man

What's good on land, good at sea and sucks up dirt?
   A hoovercraft

What colour are hiccups?
   Burple

What's round and covered in fingerprints?
   A felt hat

What's the best thing to do if you lose your head?
   Call for a headhunter.

What's Roman and climbs walls?
   IV

What's got twelve letters and is found at the bottom of an
Irish milk bottle?
   OPEN OTHER END

What made the jelly wobble?
It saw the milk shake.

What sits on a shelf and wobbles?
Jellyvision

What's red like an Indian, has two legs like an Indian, two
eyes like an Indian, looks like an Indian but isn't an
Indian?
   A photograph of an Indian

What's tall, green and very wrinkled?
   The Incredible Hulk's granny

What's sweet and musical?
   I-sing sugar

What's a man with a car on his head called?
  Jack

What's a sick joke?
  Something that shouldn't be brought up in conversation

What's sweet and wobbles through the air?
  A jelly-copter

What's covered with cream and lives in the sea?
  A jelly fish

What sits in a pram and wobbles?
  A jelly baby

What's bald and wobbles?
  Jelly Savalas

What's the best place to buy exotic plants?
  A jungle sale

What would you call a man with a jelly in one ear and a
blancmange in the other?
  A trifle deaf

  What's an ig?
    An Eskimo's house with an outside lavatory

  What's an icon?
    The fruit of an Australian oak tree

What did King John wear?
  Nothing. He lost everything in the Wash.

What makes Lucy Lucky?
  'K'

What's hot and goes 'Hoot, hoot'?
  Kentucky Fried Owl

What happened when the karate champion joined the army?
　　He saluted an officer and killed himself.

What's good for water on the kneee?
　　A tap on the ankle

What's a neurotic young goat called?
　　A crazy mixed-up kid

What's big, hairy, and flies at the speed of sound?
　　King Concorde

What's a bald detective with a camera called?
　　A Kojak instamatic

What's a hungry mathematician's favourite food?
　　Anything as long as it's a square meal

What's yellow and lands in scrap yards?
　　A Japanese kamikaze pilot with a homing device in the engine

　　What's Kojak's favourite washing powder?
　　　　Bald Automatic

　　What part of Britain has the stupidest people?
　　　　London – that's where the population is the densest

　　What's close to silver and cheeky?
　　　　The Lone Ranger's bottom

　　What's the best thing to do if you find a lion under your bed?
　　　　Sleep somewhere else.

What's short, scared of wolves, and swears a lot?
　　Little Red Riding Rude

What's small, irritating, and used after a bath?
　　A little thing that's sent to dry us

What's green and leaves the ground at 100 miles an hour?
　　A lettuce elan

What's masked and lends money?
  The lone arranger

What happened to the boy with the photographic memory?
  Nothing! It didn't develop.

What's open when it's shut and shut when it's open?
  A level crossing

What's half a tonne, travels a 70 miles an hour, and drips?
  An articulated lolly

What's small, French and clean?
  Two-loos Lautrec

What has two heads, one tail, with four legs on one side
and two on the other?
  A horse being ridden side-saddle

What's white, speaks French, and runs at 60 miles an hour?
  A lying Frenchman

What's grey and runs round buses at 100 miles an hour?
  A lightning conductor

What's yellow and deadly?
  Chop-sueycide

What's full of holes and holds water?
  A wet sponge

What's a musical insect?
  A humbug

What's green, bent, and indestructible?
  The Six Million Dollar Cucumber

What's good for nervous elephants?
  Trunkquillizers

What's brown, smelly and sounds like a bell?
  Dung

What's a mischievous egg called?
  A practical yolker

What's a man with a paper hat called?
  Russell

What's wet and goes upwards?
  A backward raindrop

What's a horse that left its stable called?
  A refugee-gee

What has feathers and stands in the middle of the road?
  A Rhode Island Red

What's the best way to stop a rooster crowing on Monday?
  Eat it on Sunday.

What's a spider doing in a bowl of alphabet soup?
  Learning to read

What's a fly doing in a bowl of alphabet soup?
  The breast stroke

What's the bluebottle doing in a bowl of alphabet soup?
  Drowning!

What's a transparent Scotsman called?
  A plastic mac

What's after the Stone Age and the Bronze Age?
  The Saus-Age

What's the quickest way to the railway station?
  Run as fast as you can.

What's a rude ram?
Very non-ewe

What's white and goes 'Baa-baa splat'?
  A sheep falling off a cliff

What's Welsh and moves traffic?
  A Dai-version

What has two legs, one wheel and smells?
  A barrowful of manure

What's got seven letters and is always spelt wrongly?
  'Wrongly!'

Loony fruit and veg

What's sweet and sour and served for pudding?
Apple grumble

What's red and green and wears boxing gloves?
A fruit punch

What's the favourite pudding in Wales?
Taffy apples

What's yellow and flashes?
A banana with a loose connection

What's yellow and always points north?
A magnetic banana

What's yellow and always points south?
An Irish magnetic banana!

What's brown, mad and lives in South America?
A Brazil nut

What's green on the outside and yellow inside?
A banana disguised as a cucumber

What's yellow, strong and very expensive?
A bunch of bionic bananas

What's yellow and square?
A banana in disguise

What's purple and frightens people?
Frankengrape

What's green, hairy and takes aspirin?
    A gooseberry with a hangover

What's purple and 8,000 kilometres long?
    The Grape Wall of China

What's purple and conquered the world?
    Alexander the Grape

What's purple and close to France?
    Grape Britain

What's purple and crackles?
    A grape that's not wired up properly

What's purple and glows in the dark?
    A 200-watt grape

What's purple and divides USA and Canada?
    The Grape Lakes

What's a goose's favourite fruit?
    Gooseberries, of course!

What's green, hairy, and drinks out of the wrong side of
the cup?
    A gooseberry with hiccups

What's yellow and 449 metres high?
    The Empire State Banana

What's yellow and wears a mask?
  The Lone Banana

What's yellow and goes 'Click, click, slip'?
  A ball-point banana

What do you get if you cross a banana with a skunk?
  A skunk with a yellow streak down its back

What did the banana do when the chimpanzee chased it?
  The banana split

What do you get if you cross a banana with a comedian?
  Peels of laughter

What's fruity and burns cakes?
Alfred the Grape

What's green and dangerous?
Angry apples

What's green and goes 'Bang, bang, bang, bang'?
  A four-door apple

What's the best time to pick apples?
  When the farmer is in bed

What do you get if you cross an apple with an alligator?
  An apple that bites you before you can bite it

What do you get if you cross an apple with a shellfish?
  A crab apple

What's yellow and good at sums?
   A banana with a calculator

What's yellow, washable and doesn't need ironing?
   A drip-dry banana

What's yellow and goes 'Beep, beep, b. .e. . .ee. . . .e. . .'?
   A lemon with a broken horn

What's yellow and goes round and round and round?
   A long-playing lemon

What's red and goes up and down, up and down, up and
down, up and down?
   A tomato in a lift

What's red, full of seeds and looks like half a tomato?
   The other half of a tomato

What's green and weighs 20 kilogrammes?
   A plumpkin

What's purple and orbits the Sun?
The Planet of the Grapes
What's rhubarb?
Celery that's boiling mad.

What would you get if you crossed a lemon with a dinosaur?
   A dino-sour

What's yellow and sweet and holds baby monkeys?
   An ape-ricot

What's an apple that is small and yellow at picking time?
  A failure

What's yellow, sour and goes 'Splutter, splutter, splutter'?
  A lemon running out of juice

What's brown, hairy and croaks?
  A coconut with a cold

What's purple and ruled Russia?
  Catherine the Grape

What's purple and burns?
  The Grape Fire of London

WHO'S DA FADDER O' THIS THEN?

What did the chicken say when it found a lemon in the nest?
  'Look at the lemon-mama-laid.' (Lemon marmalade)

What's brown, hairy and doesn't go out much?
  A coconut shy

What's worse than finding a maggot in your apple?
  Finding half a maggot in your apple!

What's furry, whiskered and sucks lemons?
  A sour puss

What hangs on a tree and shouts 'Help!'?
  A damson in distress

What did the grape say when the elephant trod on it?
  Nothing. It just gave out a little whine.

What did the elephant say to the lemon?
  'Let's play squash'.

Oh no! Not another elephant joke

What did the river say when the elephant sat in it?
  'Well, I'll be damned.'

What's grey, has a trunk and takes off from Heathrow?
  A jumbo jet

What time is it when an elephant sits on your car?
  Time to get a new car

What stopped the two elephants going for a swim on a hot day?
  They only had one pair of trunks between them.

What's best for a blue elephant?
  A trip to the circus to cheer him up

What's got four legs and flies?
  An elephant that's been dead for a month

What's bright blue and weighs 4 tonnes?
  An elephant holding its breath

What do elephants use to talk to each other?
  'elephones

What made the elephant leave the circus?
  It was fed up with working for peanuts.

What's grey, weighs 4 tonnes and lives in California?
  An L.A. phant

What's 4 tonnes in weight, has a trunk and is bright red?
  An embarrassed elephant

What's grey, weights 4 tonnes and wears glass slippers?
  Cinderelephant

What's 2 foot long, has thirty-two eyes and two tongues?
  An elephant's sneakers

What's grey weighs 4 tonnes and goes 'Clump, clump, swish, swish'?
  An elephant with flippers on its back feet

What's grey, weighs 4 tonnes and plays squash?
  An elephant in a phone box

What's grey, weighs 4 tonnes and flies?
  An elephant in a helicopter

What was the elephant doing on the M1?
  About 10 miles an hour

What do you get if you cross an elephant with Mrs Thatcher?
  An even bigger bully

What animals took longest to get to the Ark?
  The elephants – they had to pack their trunks.

What's an elephant in a 'fridge called?
  A very tight squeeze

What's yellow, weighs 4 tonnes and has a blocked trunk?
  An elephant drowning in a bowl of custard

What's black and found between elephant's toenails?
  Slow natives

What's got four ears, eight legs, two tails, four eyes and two trunks?
  An elephant with spare parts

What's the best way to get five elephants in a Mini?
  Two in the front, two in the back and one in the glove
  compartment

What's the best way to get twenty elephants in a Mini?
  Cremate them and put the ashes in the ashtray.

What's red, weighs 4 tonnes and sits in a cherry tree?
  An elephant disguised as a cherry

What did the elephant say to her naughty child?
  'Tusk! Tusk!'

What's feathered and crossed the Alps on elephants?
  Hannibal's army

What did the peanut say to the elephant?
  Nothing. Peanuts can't talk.

What's grey, weighs 4 tonnes and leaves footprints in
the butter?
  An elephant in the 'fridge

What do you give a seasick elephant?
  Plenty of room

What's pink, slimy and weighs 4 tonnes?
  An insideout elephant

What's the best thing to do if an elephant charges?
  Pay and run

What's grey and makes you touch the ceiling?
  An elephant under your bed

What's white on the outside, grey in the middle and heavy in your stomach?
  An elephant sandwich

What do elephants say when they bump into each other?
  'Small world, isn't it?'

What's a hitch-hiking elephant called?
  Stranded

What's grey, weighs 4 tonnes and jumps higher than a house?
  An elephant! Houses can't jump.

What's grey, heavy and sings jazz?
  Elephants Gerald

Vive la difference one more time

What's the difference between an Indian elephant and an African elephant?
  About 3,000 kilometres

What's the difference between an elephant and spaghetti?
  Elephants don't slip off the end of your fork.

What's the difference between a garden sprinkler and a washerwoman?
  One keeps the lawn wet: the other keeps the laun-dry.

What's the difference between a greedy person and a grill?
  One takes most: the other makes toast.

What's the difference between a monkey and an idiot?
  You can hold a conversation with a monkey.

What's the difference between a small witch and a deer?
  One is a stunted hag: the other is a hunted stag.

What's the difference between a train and a teacher?
  One goes 'choo-choo': the other says 'Take that gum out of your mouth'.

What's the difference between stork and butter?
  Butter can't stand on one leg.

What's the difference between an angry audience and a cow with a bad throat?
  One boos madly: the other moos badly.

What's the difference between a dinosaur and a sandwich?
  A sandwich doesn't weigh 5 tonnes.

'What's the difference between a dinosaur and a snew?'
  'What's snew?'
  'Not a lot. What's new with you'

What's the difference between a fisherman and a naughty schoolboy?
  One baits his hooks: the other hates his books.

What's the difference between a unicorn and a large lettuce?
One is a funny beast: the other is a bunny feast.

What's the difference between an exhausted hiker and a man on the telephone?
One is a tired walker: the other is a wired talker.

What's the difference between a man who makes £5 notes and a glutton?
One is a good forger: the other is a food gorger.

What's the difference between a fidget and a bankrupt?
One can't settle down: the other can't settle up.

What's the difference between a super policeman and a traffic-light?
One is a star copper: the other is a car stopper.

What's the difference between pack-ice and a clothes brush?
One crushes boats: the other brushes coats.

What's the difference between a schoolboy and an engine-driver?
One has a mind to train: the other has a train to mind.

What's the difference between a hungry man and a greedy one?
One longs to eat: the other eats too long.

What's the difference between a thief and church bells?
One steals from people: the other peals from steeples.

What's the difference between the North Pole and the South Pole?
That's a question of degrees.

What's the difference between a cloud and a man standing on a drawing-pin?
One pours with rain: the other roars with pain.

'What's the difference between a £5 note and a lettuce?'
  'I don't know.'
  'You couldn't lend me a lettuce, could you?

What's the difference between a mirror and a gossip?
  One speaks without reflection: the other reflects without
  speaking.

What's the difference between Italian grapes and Scots
ones?
  The Italian ones have a better suntan

What's the difference between a Boeing 747 and a lemon?
  A lemon can't cross the Atlantic without refuelling.

What's the difference between a sailor and a bargain-
hunter?
  One sails the seas: the other sees the sales.

'What the difference between a pound and the ocean?'
  'I don't know. What's the difference between a pound and
  the ocean?'
  'Weight and sea!'

What's the difference between a newspaper and a TV?
Have you ever tried swotting a fly with a TV?

What's the difference between an oak tree and tight shoes?
  One makes acorns: the other makes corns ache.

What's the difference between a jeweller and a goaler?
  One sells watches: the other watches cells.

What's the difference between a tailor and a horse trainer?
  One tends mares; the other mends tears.

What's the difference between a composer and a postman?
  One writes notes: the other delivers them.

What's the difference between a young lady and a fresh
loaf?
  One is a well-bred maid: the other is well-made bread.

What's the difference between an ice cream and a bully?
  You lick one: the other licks you.

A little eavesdropping

What did Adam say to his wife on 24 December?
'It's Christmas Eve.'

What did the man say when he walked into a bar?
'Ouch!'

What did the right rugby boot say to the left rugby boot?
'Between us we'll have a ball.'

What were Anne Boleyn's last words?
'I think I'll go for a walk around the block.'

What did the bus-conductor say to the one-legged passenger?
'Hop on!'

What did Cinderella say when her holiday snaps were late?
'Some day my prints will come.'

What did the cucumber say to the jam jar?
'If you'd kept your mouth shut, I wouldn't be in this pickle.'

What did the cat say when it was run over?
'I don't have the guts to do anything about it!'

What did the calculator say to the geometry book?
'Between us we've got a lot of problems.'

What did the carpet say to the desk?
'I can see your drawers.'

What did the big chimney say to the little chimney?
'You're far too young to smoke.'

What did the electricity meter say to the 10p piece?
'Glad you dropped in. I was just going out.'

What did the cashier say to the adding machine?
'I'm counting on you.'

What did the chocolate say to the lollipop?
'Hello sucker.'

What did the biscuit say when it was run over?
'Oh crumbs!'

What did the macramé expert say to the string?
'Get notted.'

What did the doctor say to the Invisible Man?
'Next please.'

What did the mayonnaise say to the 'fridge?
'Shut the door. I'm dressing.'

What did the flea say to Robinson Crusoe?
'See you on Friday.'

What did the flea say to the other flea?
'Shall we walk or take the cat?'

What did the big hand say to the little hand?
'Got a minute?'

What did the little hand say to the big hand?
'See you on the hour.'

What did Hamlet say to weight-watchers?
'Tubby or not tubby?'

What did the doctor say to the Invisible Man's wife?
'I can't see anything wrong with your husband.'

What does the sea say to the sand?
  Not a lot. It usually waves.

What did the stocking say to the shoe?
  'See you soon: I've gotta run.'

What did the big toe say to the little toe?
  'Don't look now: we're being followed by a couple of
  heels.'

What did the traffic light say to the car?
  'Don't look while I'm changing.'

What did one tonsil say to the other tonsil?
  'It must be spring: here comes a swallow.'

What did the tonic water say to the gin?
  'I'm diluted to meet you.'

What did the nun say as she crossed the zebra crossing?
  'Now you see me: now you don't.'

What did the pencil say to the rubber?
  'Take me to your ruler.'

What did one ear say to the other ear?
  'Between you and me we need a haircut.'

What did the carrot say to the potato?
  'Stop making eyes at me.'

What did the painter say to the wall?
  'One more crack like that and I'll plaster you.'

What did the strawberry say to the other strawberry?
  'If we hadn't been in bed together, we wouldn't be in this
  jam.'

What did the wall say to the plug?
  'Socket to me baby.'

What did one handcuff say to the other handcuff?
  'Why don't you join me.'

What did the arthritis say to the rheumatism?
  'Let's get out of this joint.'

What did the jack say to the car?
  'Wanna lift?'

What did the launch pad say to the rocket?
  'Clear off – you're fired!'

What did the frankfurter say to the ketchup?
  'That's enough of your sauce.'

What did the scissors say to the paper?
  Something very cutting

What did the soil say to the rain?
  'Stop or my name is mud.'

What did the necklace say to the crown?
  'You go on ahead: I'll hang around.'

What did the right eye say to the left eye?
  'Between ourselves, there's something that smells.'

What did one sheik say to the other sheik?
  'Oil see you again.'

What did the puddle say to the rain?
  'Drop in sometime.'

What did the digital watch say to the alarm clock?
'Look no hands.'

What did the mother worm say to the baby worm?
'You're late. Where on earth have you been?'

What did the coke sing to the coal?
'What kind of fuel am I?'

What did the squirrel say to his girlfriend?
'I'm nuts about you'

What did the raindrop say to the others?
'Two's company: three's a cloud.'

What did the appendix say to the kidney?
'The doctor's taking me out tonight.'

What did the bee say to the rose?
'Hi bud.'

What did the rose say to the bee?
'Buzz off.'

What did the brush say to the vacuum cleaner?
'Heard the latest dirt?'

What did the queen bee say to the naughty drone?
'Behive yourself.'

What did Little John say when Robin Hood fired at him by mistake?
'That was an arrow escape.'

What did the alarm clock say to the rain?
'Stop. I'm ringing wet.'

What did the wood say to the drill?
'Go away. You bore me.'

What did the window say to the venetian blind?
'If it wasn't for you it'd be curtains for me.'

What did the girl watch say to the boy watch?
'Keep your hands to yourself.'

What did the North wind say to the South wind?
'Want a game of draughts?'

What did the snooker ball say to the other snooker ball?
'Don't move until you get your cue.'

What did the doctor say to the pale orange?'
'You look off-colour; are you peeling well?'

What did the religious carrot say to the greens?
'Lettuce pray.'

The Irish never speak well of one another (Dr Johnson)

So why should we? (Ed)

What's dead and climbs walls?
  An Irish ghost

What's the best way to keep an Irishman happy?
  Give him a piece of paper with PTO printed on both sides.

What's found in Dublin and called 'Spot'?
  An Irishman's pet zebra

What happened when the Irishman changed his mind?
  His new one didn't work either.

What happened when the Irishman tried to blow up a bus?
  He burnt his mouth on the exhaust pipe.

What takes off in New York and lands in Paris?
  An Aer Lingus flight to Dublin

What happened to the Irish sea scout?
  His tent sank

What happened to the Irish tap dancer?
  He broke his leg when he fell in the sink.

What happened to the Irishman when he put some toilet water on after shaving?
  He was knocked out when the lavatory seat fell on his head.

What's small, crawls and chews bricks?
  An Irish woodworm

What sits at a piano spinning round and round?
  An Irishman trying to play the piano stool

What goes into shops and puts things back on the shelves?
  An Irish kleptomaniac

What do you get if you cross a monkey with an Irishman?
  A stupid monkey

What made the Irishman cross the road?
  He wanted to get to the middle.

What's 5 metres long with an IQ of 50?
  Fifty Irishmen in a bus queue

What's green and served hot straight from the oven?
  An Irish salad

What's got four letters and is found at the top and bottom of an Irish stepladder?
  'Stop'

What's 10 foot tall and lives in Dublin?
  Paddy Long Legs

What did the Irish spy do when he found his room was bugged?
  Sprayed it with DDT

What happened to the Irish glass-blower?
  He inhaled and got a pane in his stomach.

What's white and runs backwards in slow motion?
  The Six Million Dollar Irishman

At cross purposes again

What do you get if you cross a chicken with a banjo?
    A self-plucking chicken

What do you get if you cross a magician with a helicopter?
    A flying sorcerer

What do you get if you cross a hyaena with an oxo cube?
    An animal that makes a laughing stock of itself

What do you get if you cross a rabbit with a spider?
    A harenet

What do you get if you cross a cowboy with a stew?
    Hopalong Casserole

What do you get if you cross a baby, a soldier and an electric bulb?
    A member of the light infant-ry

What do you get if you cross an iceberg with an alligator . . .?
    A cold snap

. . . and an iceberg with a witch?
    A cold spell

What do you get if you cross a germ with a comedian?
    Sick jokes

What do you get if you cross a grammar school with Sir Lancelot?
    A knight school

What do you get if you cross a kangaroo with a sheep?
    A woolly jumper

What do you get if you cross a hyaena with a mynah bird?
    An animal that laughs at its own jokes

What do you get if you cross a stream and a river?
    Wet feet

What do you get if you cross an old Egyptian with a door bell?
　　Toot-en-come-in

What do you get if you cross a flat fish with George Washington?
　　The flounder of the USA

What do you get if you cross Dracula with a dwarf?
　　A vampire that bites kneecaps

What do you get if you cross a microphone with a dressing-gown?
　　A mike-robe

What do you get if you cross David Coleman with a potato?
　　A common-tator!

What do you get if you cross a mynah bird with a homing pigeon?
　　A bird that can ask its way home if it gets lost

What do you get if you cross a policeman with a tree?
　　A member of the special branch

What do you get if you cross an encyclopedia with a pair of trousers?
　　Smarty pants

What would you get if you crossed a watch dog with a werewolf?
    Very nervous postmen

What do you get if you cross an angry comic with rolls straight from the oven?
    Hot cross puns

What do you get if you cross a pig with a naked runner?
    Streaky bacon

What do you get if you cross a policeman with Terry Wogan?
    An arresting personality

What do you get if you cross a porcupine with a mole?
    Tunnels that leak

What do you get if you cross a pop-singer with a seat?
    A rocking chair

What do you get if you cross a railway engine with chewing-gum?
    A chew-chew train

What do you get if you cross a thief with an orchestra?
    Robbery with violins

What do you get if you cross a skunk with an eagle?
    An animal that stinks to high heaven

What do you get if you cross a pig with a motorway?
    A road hog

What do you get if you cross an idiot with a 'fridge?
    An iced wally

What do you get if you cross a glow worm with a python?
  A 20-foot long strip-light that can squeeze you to death

What would you get if you crossed an elephant with a rooster?
  An animal that wakes people who live on the top floor

What do you get if you cross an elephant with a rubber band?
  An animal that never forgets snap decisions

What would you get if you crossed an elephant with a computer?
  A big know-all

What would you get if you crossed an elephant with a skunk?
  A big stinker

What do you get if you cross a racehorse with a giraffe?
  An animal that's difficult to ride but great in a photo-finish

What do you get if you cross a cow with an Arab?
  A milk sheik

What would you get if you crossed a racing driver with a butterfly?
Stirling Moth

What do you get if you cross a chicken with an electric organ?
Hammond eggs

What do you get if you cross a chicken with a waitress?
Neatly laid eggs

What do you get if you cross an elephant with the abominable snowman?
A jumbo-Yeti